A Life Worth Living

Shannon Stephens

Shannon Stephens

WestBow
PRESS

A DIVISION OF THOMAS NELSON

WestBow Press books may be ordered through booksellers or by contacting:

WestBow Press
A Division of Thomas Nelson
1663 Liberty Drive
Bloomington, IN 47403
www.westbowpress.com
1-(866) 928-1240

Because of the dynamic nature of the Internet, any web addresses or links contained in this book may have changed since publication and may no longer be valid. The views expressed in this work are solely those of the author and do not necessarily reflect the views of the publisher, and the publisher hereby disclaims any responsibility for them.

Any people depicted in stock imagery provided by Thinkstock are models, and such images are being used for illustrative purposes only.

Certain stock imagery © Thinkstock.

ISBN: 978-1-4497-6686-3 (sc)
ISBN: 978-1-4497-6687-0 (e)

Library of Congress Control Number: 2012918139

Printed in the United States of America

WestBow Press rev. date: 9/28/12

First of all I would like to give Glory to God for helping me make this book a reality. I hope it shows how AWESOME God truly is. Second I dedicate this book to my loving family and friends. To my wonderful husband Travis, who never left me and has always been by my side, thank you & I love you! Next to my beautiful children Jordyn, Macy, Zach and step daughter Brooke, watching you grow in your relationship with Christ is a true blessing. Please know how much we love you and you are a true blessing to your father and me every day. Finally, to my dearest friends and family, I can't thank you enough for being there for us always in good times & bad. We love you! We thank God for Blessing us with all of you, you are a true gift from God.

Always remember: **Philippians 4:13** "*I can do ALL things through Christ who strengthens me.*"

Wishing you all the best, in His love,

Shannon Stephens

1

Living a life in and out of mayhem had been my life since my life began. Makes you question what the purpose of my life was that made it worth living. Being out of the home since age 9 after my father's demonstrated lack of commitment to his marriage while breaking up the family made me wonder what my life had in store. We went to church so I also struggled with the concept of a "loving father".

Before the divorce our family struggled as my father didn't know 2 things, how to be a dad and how to control his temper. He tormented my older brother until a major incident happened and after that I became the object for his anger and frustration.

When my parents decided to get a divorce on my 9th birthday little did I know that my struggle with life was only just beginning. My first step father was out on a mission. After securing a relationship with my mother he decided it was time to eliminate what he didn't want to deal with, her children. He was often a wild roller-coaster of emotions and a troublemaker prior to meeting my mom. After having 2 more kids with my mom as he struggled with the relationship and made a series of bad choices that left my mom and me in several difficult situations.

After years of craziness and drama I finally ended up in states custody and in a foster home. I was blessed to have been put in a loving & caring home, with Ron & Julia Weeks, where I was made part of their family and considered one of theirs. Whenever you hear me refer to mom & dad this is who I am talking about. The drama with my own family didn't stop there. On my 8th grade graduation my biological mom pulled a 12 gauge shotgun on my grandma and younger siblings instead of coming to celebrate my promotion into high school. My biological father just kept getting married and divorced making empty promises and was never there.

After trying to live with my biological mom one last time I spent the rest of my childhood in foster care until age 16 when I was emancipated. Then I spiraled downwards making one bad decision after another by getting pregnant and miscarrying twins my junior year to getting married right after high school into a bad relationship. I was on the wrong way path in my life where my situation only got worse before better.

The Lord blessed me with 2 beautiful daughters, but I had not yet seen His plan or was living His way. I was caught in a continuous circle of deception and terrible treatment from friends, family and husband. It took my daughter being placed in an awful situation before I finally decided I was done and this part of my life was over because I was getting out. After securing the safety of my daughters I relocated to try to re-start our lives. Little did I know that the worst was yet to come!

2

I was still not living my life the way God wanted. I was dating, having one night stands, plus trying to take care of my girls, work & go to school. I put a single's ad online and little did I know then that God would use that to get me to where He wanted me in a way I would never understand. I met my husband through the online singles ad. It was February 13, 2002 when we first met face to face. It was the night before he had started to snag my heart.

We were talking on the phone for about 5 to 6 hours. Through my homework and supper to giving kids a bath. The first thing that got me was that he had custody of his daughter that he adopted from his first marriage. He sealed the deal when it was getting late and I was getting tired and we were still talking. I told him I was going to have to get to bed unless he was going to sing me to sleep. That's when he asked me what I wanted to hear and I just told him to surprise me. He then started singing "Baby Blue" by George Strait and just melted my heart. We met the next day at a restaurant and things started to bloom from there.

I was living in the city and Travis, my husband, is a farmer, enjoying the country life. I had decided earlier before meeting him that I didn't want my kids going to school in the city. I was from a small town and wanted that for my girls. I didn't realize it then that God had already begun working His magic in my life.

My girls were just 3 & 4 when we met. Things just took off between Travis & I. Eventually ending up with my girls and I moving in with him. This again not in accordance with God's will as we should have been married first.

It was in mid-May 2002 when Travis proposed to me, which I gladly accepted. It was really neat the way he went about it. He took us to Town East Mall in Wichita. There they have an indoor carrousel where he planned to pop the question, but we didn't make it that far. We had only gotten a way inside the mall when we came up on a little photo booth. The girls wanted to get in with all of us and take pictures. The whole proposal played out in each picture. The 4 pictures that printed on the black and white strip started with the girls in front and Travis and I in the back facing each other. Then you see the box in his hand behind his back. The next frame showed the box opened presenting it to me and the last frame showed him putting on the ring and you could tell we were kissing as all the girls were looking at us in the last picture. A total of 4 pictures that would forever hold the step by step proposal on film, it was priceless.

The first Sunday after becoming engaged I went to church with him and asked his preacher if he would marry us. I was so excited that my fairy tale dream was finally coming true. But there was a lot left to come.

It was the morning of June 5, 2002, that's when my life would change forever. Travis and I had woke up, been a little intimate that morning then he was getting ready to go to work. As he got up he said something to me. When I tried to respond only jumble came out. He thought I was just joking around and told me to knock it off, but I was getting scared because I couldn't get my words to come out right. He turned to look at me and I tried to get up and couldn't. Freaking out and my adrenaline kicking in, I stood up only to fall over right into the closet. He picked me up off the floor and I communicated to him to get me to the bathroom, not sure what that was going to do, but he did and I fell off the toilet. He then picked me up and took me in and laid me on the bed and was going to call 9-1-1 but I wouldn't let him. So I agreed to let him call his mom who was a R.N. and she came straight over. She took one look at me and asked me to smile. I shot her what I thought was my best smile but only half of my face moved. She instantly got on the phone and the ambulance was there.

We live in a small farm community in Norwich, KS and so they asked where they wanted them to take me, to Kingman or to Wichita. They decided to take me to Kingman. They called in that they were bringing a 23 yr. old probable stroke victim in. I will never forget the ride there because they all kept telling me to do was stay awake and keep my eyes open and stay with them. All that I could think of is that if I closed my eyes I would die, and that's when it hit me if I died where I would go. Well it wasn't communicated to the EMT's that Kingman had no MRI machine to check to see if there was a clot or a bleed.

Upon arriving at Kingman there was nothing they could do for me there so they called life flight in. I couldn't communicate much vocally but was able to communicate on paper the names and phone numbers of my parents/family which Travis's mom called and notified them of the situation. In Kingman I was still able to wiggle my toes and move my leg. The wait seemed forever.

Life flight arrived and got me loaded in the chopper and they told me I could rest they would be there in no time. All I could think of was what the EMT's that kept telling me to stay awake and there was no way I was going to sleep now. Arriving in Wichita, KS at St. Francis Hospital, they rushed me right into the MRI and scanned my brain. At this point it was found to be a clot but too late to give me the clot buster medication and by this time I had lost movement of my left leg, my left arm was unmovable in Kingman.

They got me upstairs into ICU and my biological father came in the room. My biological mother never came. We were waiting to speak to the neurologist. The neurologist came in and I asked him when I would be able to walk and be normal again he told me that I should just be lucky that I was alive because I would never be out of a hospital bed again. He went on proceeding to tell me that I had lost 45% of my front right lobe of my brain. He continued to talk at this point I was just thinking about the fact that this doctor had just told me the rest of my life was going to be living in a hospital bed having to have consistent care. When the doctor finishing speaking to us he asked if we had any questions and Kevin, my biological father, said yes and requested a new neurologist. This doctor was giving me no hope or even a chance and so our request was granted and the hospital called in another neurologist to see me.

The new doctor looked at the test and results confirming what the first doctor had told us but with the exception that he was going to have me evaluated by therapy to see if I was even a candidate for rehab. I had to wait till I was out of ICU before that could even happen. I was in and out a lot but I was stable and able to be moved to regular room in just a couple of days.

I will never forget being moved into a regular room, Travis was consistently by my side. We were just talking when the nurse came in and told me I had a visitor. She told me that MY pastor was here to see me. This was a total shock and kind of confusing to me because I didn't have a pastor. That's when Pastor Kurt Henson walked into my room. He was Travis's pastor who I had asked earlier to marry us before my stroke. This was only the beginning of the example of what a Godly man he was and the beginning of how God was going to show himself to me through Pastor Kurt. The Bible says that we love because God first loved us. Pastor Kurt showed this to me by claiming me as my pastor when I thought I didn't have one. This was only the beginning.

The next day I was evaluated to see if I was a candidate for rehab therapy. I couldn't stand or move on my own but these two therapists came in and started working with me. One would hold me up while the other moved my feet. As they were attempting to move me around the room all I could think of was how disappointing it was because I couldn't walk without having someone moves my leg for me. I thought all was hopeless and was waiting for the bad news when they turned to Travis & me and said that I was a perfect candidate for rehab therapy and that they could feel muscles in my leg trying to fire and that I needed to be transferred into an inpatient rehab hospital as soon as possible. The next day, in my wheelchair, I was transferred to my new temporary home of the inpatient rehab hospital.

It was frustrating. Everything I knew and could do and enjoyed, I could no longer do. I couldn't even go to the bathroom alone. I loved to run, play with my girls, play piano, play basketball, cross stitch, etc., and none of that was possible for me to do anymore. I felt like I had lost myself. Plus I was newly engaged, had 2 girls of my own from my first marriage, & Travis being a farmer was in the start of wheat harvest. Little did I know that God was going to start showing Himself in all kinds of ways.

Every day I had 3 hours of therapy, 1 hour of occupational therapy, 1 hour of speech therapy and 1 hour physical therapy. I had to learn to walk all over again. My body would not listen to me. It seemed like everything I wanted it to do was impossible. It was so easy to get down and depressed. There were days I didn't want to get out of bed. God's word encourages you to get up daily and only focus on what is good. There in the beginning of therapy it was hard. It was also hard to end the day on a good note. I missed my girls terribly and Travis always had to leave to go back home to take care of the girls and meet the needs at that end too.

I was only beginning to see what a wonderful man God had put in my life as Travis was doing everything he needed to and then some. After moving him and the girls into his parents' house, he would wake up every morning and get the girls going. Then he would head out to the field and cut wheat all day long till about 6pm when he would quit and head into Wichita to come see me. After having 3 hours of therapy a day he would come in and do more with me, doing range of motion and strength training to help with my learning to walk again. Then after spending about 1 ½ to 2 hours with me he would head home to help get the girls to bed, reassuring them I was okay. He would read them a story, say a prayer and put them to bed to go to bed his self to get up and do it all over again the next day. There wasn't a day that went by that I didn't see him.

Therapy was challenging daily, trying to get my body to respond. The frustration of looking at a part of your body, like your toes, and being able to wiggle the toes on one foot while the other foot did nothing. I will never forget the day I took my first step. My physical therapist was awesome and challenged me more and more each day, I took my first step and could feel my body was starting to listen to my brain and started to react. As soon as therapy was over I went and called Travis to come in. My therapist waited for him to get there before he left work for the day. After Travis finally made it in we all went into the therapy room where I stood up and took my first step. The tears just rolled out of our eyes. The tears of joy couldn't be stopped. I was witnessing God proving to me that He is the ultimate physician and had been with me all the time.

I was talking but I had dysplasia and I had an English accent. Everyone use to always ask me where I was from and they would get tickled when I told them I was born and raised in Kansas because when you heard me talk you would think that I was from England. I had also figured out how to put my make-up on and eventually was allowed to take myself to the bathroom without assistance. I was trying to get back into my normal routine as possible. I use to tell my therapist that I wished it would have affected my right side instead of my left because I am right handed. To walk you have to be able to use both legs so no matter what side was affected to walk again you would have to push both legs to move. But being right hand dominate made it easier for me to just figure out a new way to try to do things like putting on make-up. But if my right hand was affected I thought maybe it might make me work harder out of frustration to get it working again because my left hand and arm were not responding at all.

During this time though about every other day or so Pastor Kurt would also come up and visit me. He started getting me to memorize scripture starting with **Philippians 4:13** *"I can do ALL things through Christ who gives me strength."* Every time things would get hard I would repeat that over and over in my head asking God to give me the strength I needed.

While in rehab there was a truck driver, Ron, which was from Washington State and had a stroke in Newton, KS at a hotel and was brought in to the same rehab hospital I was in. I had been in the nursing field before my stroke and this man was wheeled in one evening at supper time. Because of the damage his stroke caused his food had to be pureed. As soon as he saw his tray he threw it across the room and wheeled himself back to his room which was the next door after mine. I took it upon myself to make this gentleman my project. He wheeled in the next morning for breakfast and I rolled up in my wheelchair and asked if I could join him. They brought him his tray and he started to go off on the staff. I knew they couldn't say anything to him and this man was old enough to be my father but I could just see the hurt and frustration on his face. As he proceeded to raise his voice and go to throw his tray I spoke up and asked him to calm down and explained to him that they were only trying to help him and was doing what was best for him. He may not like it but this was just the starting point for his recovery and I shared with him that God would help him through he just had to trust in Him and believe. We became good friends and each other's motivators.

Day by day went by, doing my scheduled therapy and then also working every evening with Travis as he came in regularly. Pastor Kurt also came in regularly and even brought his family up to see me. Each day I would face the challenges before me reminding myself that I could do anything as long as God was my strength and also

Romans 8:28: *God causes all things to work together for good to those who love God, to those who are called according to His purpose.* That's when I began to think about my purpose. People couldn't understand why I wasn't mad at God because of my stroke and that's when I realized that God gave me a 2nd chance. That He was bringing good out of my bad situation. That by allowing me to live I would be given a chance to get to know God and He would use me to share His message.

As each day went by I took it head on. I started wanting to be able to do something each new day that I hadn't been able to do the day before. I went from taking a few steps to being able to walk up and down a few stairs. It didn't come easy or right away but I got there. Then after being able to walk up and down a few steps with assistance I then had to do it on my own. Then when I was able to do a few steps on my own I was then taken outside to walk on uneven surfaces, rocks, & gravel. I was doing it first with help then on my own. I was still restricted to using my wheelchair when I wasn't in therapy but little by little I was gaining more with each day.

My 2nd week in therapy they had Travis bring his truck in and worked with me on getting in and out of a vehicle. They started pool therapy with me, where I was able to walk back and forth across the pool. Then they set up a home visit where Travis could come and pick me up and take me home so I could try to get around my house and see what difficulties I faced at home that they could help me work on back at the hospital before I went home. Well, my first home visit wasn't a real home visit at all. My doctor granted me a home visit but I went home to watch my girls play softball. I thanked him so much for allowing me this as I missed my girls terribly and wanted so much to see them play one of their last softball games of the season. I enjoyed watching the game and was embraced by the community who showed so much support for me and my family. But then it was time to be taken back to the hospital. That was always the worst part. Whether it was just Travis or Travis with the girls, every time it was time to say good bye it felt just like my heart was getting ripped out. Travis didn't bring the girls up much because it was just as hard on them as it was me and him.

As I worked each day to accomplish more so I was one more day closer to gong home, little did I know that home was only going to be harder than I thought. My doctor granted me a 2nd home visit where I went back to the farm and ate and spent time with the girls and Travis's family. It was decided that when I came home, Travis, the girls and I would move into Travis's grandparents' house which was on the farm just across the drive from his mom and dad's house where they would be close enough to help as needed.

While in recovery I had learned that one of my best friends from high school was getting married on the 7th of July. I promised her I would be there and I was shooting for that goal. So I had gone into inpatient rehab about the 10th of June in a wheel chair unable to walk, barely talk, & unable to move my arm. On July 2, 2002, I walked out of the rehab hospital on my own 2 feet heading home with Travis to get back into my life. Little did I know that this was going to be a rude awakening!

3

Things had been great in rehab. I thought I had accomplished so much and was ready to take on the world. Little did I know the world was waiting for me and ready to deal me a big blow! The first couple of days home were good as Travis was with me. But it was time for regular life to get going, & I wasn't ready for the smack in the face that I would be facing. It was the first day by myself with all 3 girls as Travis went back to work farming which is a full time job.

I love my kids more than anything but they are still kids. They were arguing and fighting and I went into the room to try to deal with it. As I stepped into the room and tried to handle what was going on one of the girls yells "just run, she can't catch you!" I tried to follow and deal with what had just happened all 3 girls ran 3 different directions. After a few minutes I gave up. Then I went into the kitchen and tried to fix something to eat for everyone but I couldn't open cans and had to use my mouth as a second hand to open anything else. Then I went to put something in the oven and my left hand dropped onto the oven door. The oven was preheated to like 400 degrees and I couldn't feel it when my hand landed on the door till it had set there a little over a minute as I was trying to maneuver food in and out of the oven. By the time I finally felt the heat on my hand I had seriously burned it. Then another argument between the girls broke out and they ran again from me.

This was it. I couldn't handle one more thing. I called Travis on his cell and asked him to come home. I was a bumbling crying mess. He came home to find me sitting on the front steps in tears. I begged him to take me back to the hospital. I just couldn't handle this life anymore. I didn't know what to do. I had it in my head that I could handle anything when I was in the hospital but once home and reality hit me in the face I just crumbled.

It was like I had forgotten where to get my strength from and was trying to do it all by myself. I started daily getting up and asking God to get me through that day and guide me and give me the strength I needed.

The girls were acting out just because they didn't know what else to do. It was a whole new life for them too. They wanted things out of me that I couldn't do anymore. I couldn't French braid their hair and put it up anymore. I struggled with house work. Before my stroke I would get up and get everyone up and dressed and day started. Then I got all the house work done including dishes, laundry, beds made, & vacuuming by noon & would go outside and hang and play with the girls the rest of the day until it was time to go in and make supper and then get everyone baths and to bed. Then Travis and I use to go for short walks or just sit outside and talk.

That was all before my stroke. Now it took 15 minutes to just open a can or package to make something to eat. It was more than frustrating when it came to laundry because it would take so long having to lay each piece of clothing out then manipulate it with one hand to try to fold it. Having to use my mouth as a second hand and eat socks to match them up as a folded pair. I couldn't even fix my own hair, which was to my shoulder blades. I had to have help for everything it seemed and the shock of it all was almost unbearable. I didn't want to cut my hair short I didn't want to accept the fact that the person I had been for the first 23 years of my life physically wasn't there anymore. What do I do now? How do I start over? I don't want to disappoint my kids or let them down but it was slowly happening. Day by day I struggled more as my girls would go to Travis or Grandma to do things that I always use to do. They didn't know how to react around me. I didn't even know how to act around myself.

I kept my promise to my best friend from high school and I made it to her wedding. I was there physically but inside I felt lost. Travis was with me. We sat down in the back of the church. I didn't dress up because I couldn't wear dress shoes anymore because my left foot was paralyzed from the ankle down and had drop foot and couldn't keep a dress shoe on. It was a beautiful ceremony and after at the reception I went up and gave her a hug and let her know that I was there.

We had taken the girls out to mom & dad's when we went to the wedding. Heading back out there after the ceremony to stay the night, the girls were all excited to see Grandma Julie & Grandpa Ron. As we headed up to bed I realized I hadn't brought my medication with me. Since my stroke I had been put on a number of medications for different reasons but one of the main ones were for my muscle spasms and chronic pain that they caused. After realizing that I had not brought my meds I tried to just live through what my body was doing because we were planning on going home the next day.

My body starting reacting to not having my meds as my left arm and leg started to flop like a fish due to continuous muscle spasms. I tried to make myself go to sleep and ignore what my body was doing but Travis could see that it wasn't getting any better. By the time we decided that there was no way I could go any longer without my meds it was after midnight. My girls were exhausted so we agreed with Mom & Dad to leave them there and that Travis and I were going to head home to get my medications and come back in the morning. That was easier said than done as when I went to get up and go down the stairs to go home my muscles were such spasms that I couldn't walk. Dad and Travis carried me down the stairs and put me into the vehicle as Mom reassured the girls that I was going to be okay. Travis and I headed home which was a little over an hour away.

Not only did my body suffer from uncontrollable spasms that required medications to control. My body on my left side also couldn't tell the difference between hot & cold. All it felt was just pain. If I wasn't looking at someone when they touched the left side of my body it felt like I was being hit with a thousand of needles. But if I watched someone touch the left side of my body then it was fine as long as I was watching it didn't hurt. It's totally weird, for lack of better term. It's like someone took a fine pen and drew a line right down the middle of my body starting at the top of my head down my face completely separating the left side from the right. I cannot begin to explain how it feels and only those who have lived through it and experience it can understand. My right side feels normal but the left side when you touch it feel like pins & needles, like when your foot has fallen asleep and you move it and that tingling feeling you feel as the blood starts flowing through it normally again. That's how it feels when my left side is touched. My left side suffered from chronic pain from all this.

Travis & I got home around 2-2:30 am when I immediately took my medication and went in and laid down. It took about 15 to 20 minutes before the medication started to help and started getting things back under control. I was finally able to get to sleep as my body was completely exhausted from all the spasms and flopping during that little over an hour drive it took us to get home. After getting some sleep Travis and I got up and headed back to Mom & Dad's to get the girls, this time with my medication. Needless to say that was a lesson it only took us once to learn from. We got up the next morning heading to Coldwater, KS; back to Mom & Dad's to get the girls. They were eagerly waiting on us, wanting to make sure I was okay.

This was all forming a new routine for what was now my new life. Taking regular medications of this nature was something I was not use to. I use to rarely take Tylenol over the counter. Now I was use to giving medication as I had worked in an assisted living home where this was my primary job.

Here I, only 23 years old, had to totally adapt to a whole new life. I didn't even know where to start. This whole situation had shaken my confidence and security to my core. Travis & I were engaged and had planned to be married in February of the following year but we decided we wanted to move the date up. So instead of waiting till February we set a new date of September 7, 2002. It was almost August so we let Pastor Kurt know right away.

Pastor Kurt encouraged us to let him do a pre-marital class/study with us before getting married. Pastor Kurt would come out once to twice a week to meet with us. I was taking in everything he said. The word of God was so interesting to me I looked forward to every meeting. Travis's mom, DeAnn, was a very strong and grounded Christian and when I wasn't talking with Pastor Kurt I was talking to her.

She used to take me to my doctor appointments. I use to get Botox injections into the deep muscles of my arm and calf muscle on my left side. I would get 20 shots at a time, getting 10 in my arm and 10 in my leg. They used that along with other medications to paralyze the muscle to try to help control the spasms. Those shots hurt but I blocked them out talking to her and learning from her about the Lord.

After many of our talks I started seriously talking with Pastor Kurt and Travis about getting baptized. Pastor Kurt encouraged me to do it before getting married. To unite myself with Christ before uniting with Travis was ideal. Travis and I were still doing pre-marital counseling as there were things we were doing that were going against God's word, which was mainly having sex before marriage. Pastor Kurt talked with me and we planned when I was going to be baptized and how. Travis was going to assist Pastor Kurt in the ceremony. I was united with Christ through baptism August 11, 2002.

After being baptized, it was like a new peace had set over me. It was something I could actually feel inside. I knew God had followed through with His word and had given me the Holy Spirit. The Bible states that the Lord watches over His word to fulfill it and I learned this myself personally.

I can only encourage everyone I know to do this. The feeling that overcomes you is completely indescribable. It's all

that the Bible says it is plus even more than I don't even know how to put into words.

This totally impacted Travis and my relationship in ways that you couldn't even begin to imagine. Being born again was literally a new start in my life in every way one could imagine. But Satan can't stand for us to have this relationship with the Lord so now that I was in this abundant glory little did I know that my new foundation was ready to be shaken. But my new found faith and relationship with God along with Travis's was going to show a miracle that was only beginning to be shown.

4

Travis and I were still doing our pre-marital counseling. Pastor Kurt was working with us to try to stay true to God's wishes for us and work within ourselves to start making the changings we needed to make so we could begin changing from the concept of being single to becoming one through God. With that being said Pastor Kurt kept reminding us of the importance of living our life now till we were married by God's rule. The main focus was acting like we were married before we were, mainly no sex before our wedding.

I woke up the next morning and my cycle had started, which us women know that is just a fact of our lives. Well normally a cycle lasts 4 to 7 days. No one wants to be intimate during that time but little did I know that this was going to be far from normal. My cycles should have been coming to its end but instead it was like someone just had turned on a faucet. I could not use enough products to keep from bleeding through everything. I was soaking bedding and the whole situation was over whelming.

Travis and his mom decided that I needed to start taking me to doctors because the situation was getting worse instead of better. None of the doctors could figure out what was going on, what was causing it or how to stop it. My blood count was dropping and I became very anemic. It was turning into a serious situation. It was within a week of our wedding and the doctors said that I had to have a blood transfusion. That I had lost so much blood that my body wasn't able to keep up with making new blood. Within that week I had 2 blood transfusions.

The big day had arrived. Travis's sister, Sherame, who was 8 months pregnant with their first child, was doing my hair. His mom, DeAnn, was making sure everything else was in place. We were getting married at the farm in his parent's backyard. They had set up this beautiful little white tent that was only big enough to cover the ceremony area. They had wrapped greenery around the poles of the tent with white Christmas lights wrapped together with it. They had set up folding chairs leaving an aisle down middle for me to walk down. My dress was a cream color antique lace looking dress that stopped at my calves. Travis's mom & sister had bought the dress many years before me thinking Sherame might wear it to a prom or something but that never happened but they never got rid of the dress thinking that one day they would find a use for it and then I came into the picture and it fit me perfectly. I was so nervous about what was going on with me medically I didn't want anything to ruin it. Travis and I had talked about it a couple days prior and he told me that I had nothing to worry about. The doctors may not be able to figure out what was going on within my body but that God was the ultimate physician and that God would show that to be. Travis told me that on our wedding night everything with me would be back to normal that God would stop the bleeding and it would gone forever and he knew it and told me to trust in that. After Travis had told me that I claimed it and put my worries to rest and anytime thoughts would come to mind or I would start to worry I would just remind myself of what Travis had said and that I had given it to God and that God had it and would just tell Satan to get out that I belonged to God and there was nothing he could do to hurt me.

My biological mom had called a few weeks before. She wasn't there for me during any time of my stroke and recovery and was now calling to let me know that she wasn't going to be there for my wedding. That she wanted no part of it. My biological dad was still around and was going to sing in my wedding but that was it. Right before the ceremony started, DeAnn, walked down and lite the candle representing his family, and my mom, Julia, walked down and lite the candle representing my family.

My 2 girls from my first marriage, Jordyn & Macy, walked me down the aisle. They gave me away to Travis. This meant the world to me because it represented to me that they gave me to Travis to be my partner in our lives and that they were also accepting him as their new father.

Our ceremony was beautiful. As I took my first step down the aisle nothing could take the smile off my face. I was walking down that aisle to the man I loved who was my best friend and hero. I was being united with him through God. Many tears were shed but I just couldn't take the smile off my face. My biological dad, Kevin, sang a song during the ceremony while we lite our unity candle. We also brought up all 3 girls, Jordyn, Macy & Brooke, and had a uniting of the family as part of our ceremony. Recognizing our family becoming 1 under God Then Travis sang a beautiful song to me. We took our first communion together as husband and wife. Then after sharing our vows and sealing it with a kiss, Pastor Kurt happily joined us as husband and wife under God with God's blessing and presented us to the crowd of our dearest friends and family as Mr. and Mrs. Travis Stephens.

After the ceremony was a reception and dance right there at the farm. We had a blast. Travis shared a mother/son dance with his mom that at that time we didn't know would be their last. Plus I got to share a dance with Kevin my biological dad as well as Ron, my dad that raised me. It was a karaoke dance so to watch the girls and other kids get up there and sing songs along with some of the Men from our congregation who sang YMCA was some of the highlights of our celebration. Then it was time to change to get ready to leave for our short planned honeymoon.

We were heading to Colorado to head out there for a little honey moon but since we got started heading that way so late we ended up spending the night in Pratt, KS for the night. I was so nervous. Even though I believed that God was going to stop the bleeding and everything that was going on with me, it was still an issue before the ceremony and before we left for Colorado. When got into our room and I voiced my concerns to Travis he just looked at me and smiled and said "Shannon, you've been healed and I'm telling you now that you no longer have any issue to be worried about.' I went into the bathroom with tears and tears instantly started streaming down my face when I saw there wasn't even a drop of blood. Everything WAS gone. God had healed me and our wedding night was perfect, only thanks to our Lord and His healing me and us believing and claiming it. Even though I was a little nervous and hesitant God showed to be that there is never a reason to doubt Him as He is the ultimate physician.

5

We had a wonderful little trip to Colorado to come home and welcome into our family exactly a month after our wedding, on October 7th, our niece was born. This was a beautiful blessing but challenges were only just ahead. After welcoming a precious little girl into this world, DeAnn was there when she was born and spent a lot of time with her in the first few months and through the holidays.

We had gotten to the beginning of a new year finding out that DeAnn had breast cancer. This was a complete shock to the whole family. Travis & I had also decided to have another baby together as he had adopted his first daughter from his first marriage then right before Christmas the adoption was final and he had adopted Jordyn & Macy too. Now with his mom facing stage 3-4 breast cancer we didn't want to lose her.

She ended up having both breasts removed and went through chemo to fight off this killer. I was pregnant but DeAnn was getting weak and sick through the treatments and so I went out every day to help her, make meals to feed the guys, and help her with anything she needed.

While helping her Sherame's husband Justin had come down to help get some farm work done. Well our Sprayer had gotten stuck and Justin had gone out in the field to help out. On his way walking out there he slipped into a hole hurting his leg. They got everything unstuck and continued work. Unfortunately though after going home Justin's leg just kept hurting and was only getting worse. So he went to the doctor to get it checked out. That's when he found out that he had bone cancer. This was such a shock to the whole family. They had just had their first baby and after finding this out they knew that their dreams for a bigger family would be out of reach because chemo and radiation makes you sterile. Justin started treatment right away.

So both DeAnn and Justin were fighting cancer at the same time. Travis already had 2 Aunts in his family that had cancer in remission and I had lost my grandma to lymphoma. A lot of prayers were going up.

Travis was a momma's boy. He and his dad had a stressed relationship but he always found comfort in his mom. Justin's treatment was working well, but DeAnn's cancer went to her liver. The doctors said that there was really nothing left for them to do so Hospice was called in. I was well into my pregnancy and was at the point where we could find out what the sex of the baby was and wanted to get it on video and share with his mom while we still could. It was a little over a month before that could happen. I continued to go out there every day and help DeAnn and with my nursing back ground I did everything I could to help out.

Travis prayed all the time for the healing of his mom and he was always telling her that she was going to be okay. She was such an example of a strong Christian woman. When it came down to where she couldn't make it to church anymore, Pastor Kurt would bring out communion and she would thank Jesus every Sunday for everything. I remember her talking to me about her concern for Travis. She told me she knew how much he was praying for her healing. She looked at me and told me to remind Travis that God is not like a genie. He hears ours prayers and decides how to answer each but that His answers may not always go along with what we want to happen. She told me she had been praying for me before she even knew me to be brought into Travis's life but that I needed to understand that God was going to answer Travis's prayer but not in the way he wants and I need to be ready to be there for him. She told me that Travis is praying to God as if He was a genie in a bottle, but He's not and God answers every prayer. Sometimes the answer is no but sometimes when the answer is yes it is yes to His plan which doesn't always match what we want. She explained that God was going to heal her by taking her home. That death sometimes is an answer to prayer. When you are praying for someone that is dying that sometimes the way God heals is to bring His own home with Him. It is selfish of us as humans to not want to lose those we love but God knows what is best and His plans are perfect even when we don't understand them.

I remember asking her if she was scared. She openly told me no. What bothered her the most was leaving the rest of us but she knew that we all knew God and he would take care of us. She told me actually she was excited because she couldn't wait to meet Christ. It may sound weird, but in a strange way, I was kind of jealous of her as she was getting to meet Jesus before the rest of us. Her overwhelming peace and strength in Christ was such a testimony. All I have ever wanted is to be an example, even in the smallest way, of the kind of Christian she was and to have the relationship she had with God. I wanted to be like that. We also talked about the baby Travis and I were going to be having. The 3D ultra sound was rescheduled and so we weren't going to be able to show her the baby. We were really upset about it and she just smiled and said that she would know what we were having before we would. She always looked to the positive of everything.

It was October 23, 2003, a beautiful morning. Sherame was there because a couple nights before we thought we were going to lose her so friends and family made a late night run up to get her to be with her mom. Her mom was over helping with the cooking because on our 5000 acre family farm there was always work to be done. This time of year the guys were in the field cutting soybeans.

It was about 11am or so and at the patio door was Pastor Kurt. Earlier the home health nurse had come in and gave a bed bath to DeAnn and not listened to my request to not change her but to just gently wash her face. We had just gotten DeAnn comfortable again because she would moan when she was in pain. This was about the time Pastor Kurt had shown up. It was just him & I in the room with DeAnn. Sherame had gone to take a shower and her mom was in the kitchen cooking. Pastor Kurt talked to DeAnn about one of her favorite Christian artist Sandi Patty and one of her favorite songs "It was a morning like this." He went on to describe to DeAnn about what a beautiful morning it was and how he believed that it was a similar morning when Jesus arose. He then told her how much she was loved but that it was okay. I was hearing the conversation but was focused in on her breathing. I had been timing her breathing and how many seconds it was before she took another breath. Pastor

Kurt looked at me and asked me "Shannon, do you know what to do?" I told him yeah but I was counting her breaths and begging her to take another. He asked me the question a second time and I was still waiting to watch her chest rise. Again for the third time he asked me the same question and then it hit me. I looked at him and said 'You mean..?" he said "Yes Shannon, she's gone home." then came the decision on whom to tell first, her mom or her daughter. I headed into the kitchen and told her mom, Louise, that she was gone. She got upset because she wanted to be in the room with her when she passed. Then I got to the bathroom door where Sherame was taking a shower. I was crying and could hardly talk by the time I got to Sherame and she opened the door and I told her the best I could that her mom was gone. She just burst into tears and went in there with her grandma. Then I had to get on the 2-way radio and call the guys in from out of the field. All I told Travis and his dad, Arland, was that they needed to get to the house right away. Travis told me as soon as he heard me and what I said he knew what had happened.

After her funeral there was a lot to be done as she was known around the world for her wheat weaving and has some of her work in the Smithsonian Museums, plus she had her shop where she sold her works of art and antiques that she had collected.

On April 6, 2004, we welcomed into our family, our son Zachary Dale Stephens. Travis's grandma said how much he looked just like DeAnn. I had made it through my high risk pregnancy without an issue. I was considered a high risk because of my stroke. They had us in the beginning of the pregnancy with Travis giving me shots for a blood thinner. We only did that for the first 3 months and then quit. Believed and had put it in God's hands that I would be fine without those shots. They regularly checked my blood and my clotting time and I was always in the normal range so we never told the doctors that we stopped taking the medicine till after Zach was delivered and they were floored. They couldn't explain how that could even be possible. We could, GOD!!!

This was going to be a whole new experience for me because when I had my girls I was normal able to use both of my hands. Now I only had one hand to use and honestly it scared me. How was I going to change a diaper, give a bath, mainly how was I going to pick him up and hold him. I was so excited to be having another baby that the reality of this didn't really hit me until I was within weeks of having him.

I knew I wasn't going to be alone and would have help. When I was 8 months pregnant I had gotten a call from my biological mom, Sue, telling me that the school had been talking with my younger sister Ashley and younger brother P.K. and that they were going to be taken out of the home and put in states custody because of situations that were going on in the home and abuse and other things the school had been seeing. So I got on the phone and talked to the social worker as well as the principal of their school and got the details and agreed to take them so they would be safe and not be in states custody. So that evening I drove up to Kansas City, Missouri and got them and brought the home. So besides Travis, I had my younger sister and the girls that could always give me a hand when needed.

But mainly Travis and I did it all, which is who it should be, but I made myself learn how to pick him up and change his diaper. I was all worked up over nothing because as things came up that needed to be done I just took my time to figure out the easiest way for me to do things. When he was first born it was easy for me to learn then I had to enhance my abilities as he got older and started moving. Dressing was one of the hard things besides changing a dirty diaper that I learned to maneuver and maneuver well. Some people would get nervous just watching me and outsiders always wanted to help or do it for me. But they learned as we all did in time that it was possible.

As time passed by, things just got easier and easier for me. Then I went to one of my follow up appointments where I saw a woman who only had one arm and 2 small children with her and expecting another one and I felt bad. That's when God humbly reminded me that when I think my life is bad there's always someone out there

Now after not quite a month after having Zach we found a rehab breakthrough in Charlotte, NC. The only down side was that I would have to fly to North Carolina alone and spend a week there, doing rehab, all alone. It look like to be a very possible way to get the use of my left hand back and even though it was incredibly tough I had to do it. I booked my flight and flew out. I had a layover in Minneapolis. Once at the airport as soon as I had to go through security I just started to cry and continued on the first flight from Wichita to Minneapolis. I didn't do anything but look out the window and cry. We landed in Minneapolis and the lady sitting beside me said "I don't know who you are or what you're going through but I have been praying for you all through this flight for God to be with you and bring you comfort." I told her thank you.

Having never been to Minneapolis airport I was completely lost and had to get clear to the other side of the airport as my connecting plane was paging me and ready to take off. There were trams and walkways and I had no clue where I was or what to do. Then all of a sudden, out of the blue, the lady from the plane was right there next to me and told me exactly what to do and how to get through the airport, what trams to take and how to catch my connecting flight. I arrived in Charlotte and took a taxi to my hotel.

I got settled in and had to be down to the conference room in my hotel by 7am to start the therapy program I was there for. As the small group of us gathered I realized that I was the only one there alone which was an eye opener making my stay there a little bit tougher. We would get done daily about 5pm and I would head up to my room and get on my laptop with my webcam and talk to my family until bedtime. The first couple of days that all I did was therapy then to my room to talk to my family. The third day, everyone wanted to have supper together and then go to the pool. I tried to not get involved but I wasn't able to stay out of it. I ended up going to the pool and there was a small group of us that were all stroke survivors with handicaps swimming together. There was a young woman there who was 16 years out from her stroke and had not gone swimming since her stroke and we got her into the water and got her swimming. I could swim under water still, not as good as when I was a kid but I did it just the same. This was amazing to some of them and that encouraged them to try. The whole experience was overwhelming to most of the other family members. I got asked a lot how I did this and that and not scared. I explained that I was scared but that I had God as my strength and that when I would doubt something or get it in my head that I couldn't do I, I would then stop, take a deep breathe, say a little prayer and try it anyway. I didn't always succeed and there was a lot of frustration at times. But I believe that God used those moments to make me stronger.

After getting home I bought what I needed to continue therapy at home with all my new knowledge and gear. I also made an appointment with my therapy doctor to go in and show them all the new stuff I had found and learned because some of what they did in the rehab hospital worked against what I had learned. That was when reality hit me in the face. At the time I had my stroke they would put the effected side in braces and have it set in certain ways. One of them was for the hand, which is what I went to N.C. for. In the hospital they would put the effected hand in what they called the "resting hand position". I learn that this actually worked against recovery as it helped shorten tendons on the arm. When I shared this information with my doctor, his response was "you have to accept the fact that you are just going to lose somethings when you have a stroke". That's when I realized that my ultimate physician was God, because man had already set limits. I continued trying to work on my hand at home but frustration and lack of improvement got the best of me and I just decided to settle.

I also had muscle spasms and chronic pain brought on from my stroke. I ended up at a pain management doctor receiving Botox injections into my arm and my leg as well as oral medications. I got injections for almost 2 years when the Botox started to quit working. My body had built up a resistance to it. I was getting 20 shots at a time, 10 into the belly of the muscle in my arm and 10 into the middle of my calf muscle. The doctors also had me on Lortabs for pain as well as an oral muscle relaxer. Since I had to quit taking the Botox I started to lean on the oral medications more. Little did I know that some of the effects of the medicines I was taking was going to come back to haunt me.

When Lortabs start to wear off they were causing ghost pains, meaning as it wears off it makes you hurt more so you will take more to get rid of the pain. At the time I did not know this, but the more you took the more pain it caused when wearing off. Thinking that I was having increasing pain I would take more and more along with muscle relaxers, I got hooked quickly. Travis had hurt his shoulder and was given Lortabs for his pain so not only was I taking my pain meds but I started taking his too. I slept most of the time, but they also made me feel warm and fuzzy along with hallucinations. I will never forget the day I was laying down in my room on my bed and I swore I heard Travis knock on the window by my head telling me he was locked out of the house. I got up and went to the door and I could see Travis but I could also see through him. This image of him walked up to me than just vanished. That totally freaked me out and I called Travis on his cell and told him about what had just happened. I knew things weren't right but I didn't know what was going on. I was missing out on my family. I wasn't making it to school events and activities. I was just there, living and breathing, but not active in any way in my life.

Pastor Kurt along with family and friends saw what was going on and tried to help him by trying to get me help. At the beginning Travis thought he could do it himself. They figured in Lortabs alone I was taking about 16 a day. He started taking my meds with him when he left the house to work on the farm and would come by when I needed my medicine and he would give me only what I was supposed to have. I went from 16 a day to 4. My body started going into withdrawal. It was Thanksgiving and I went to his family dinner but I was a mess. I was shaking and itching, begging him to take me home and give me my meds. He finally took me home, although everyone was encouraging him to get me into treatment somewhere. The next day was even worse and before noon that day I had agreed to be taken in to get help. Pastor Kurt was there and they took me to a drug rehab and admitted me. I took some clothes, my Bible, and pictures of my family. Travis and Pastor Kurt took me in got me to my room and then said their goodbyes.

I was given a tour of the place by one of the patients in there. Then back to my room where the withdrawals started happening. They gave me medicine to help take the edge off but I knew this was going to be a long night. I had been taken off all my meds till the withdrawals were over. So I had muscle spasms from my stroke plus withdrawals cause spasms as well. I laid there in bed and tried to go to sleep. I would sleep for 30-45 minutes to an hour or so then my body would literally wake me up by shaking. The pain was unbearable. I would get up and go to this little chair and table next to my bed and I would open my Bible and start reading and praying while looking at pictures of my family. The tears just rolled down my checks but then I would go back to bed and pray until I just fell asleep. This went on all night. It got to the point I could barely move and it took all I could to focus and get through it. I would have to literally pull myself into the bathroom to use it at times before laying back down. I would try to go to sleep and my left side would be flopping like a fish on dry land, then after a few minutes my right side would join in. It didn't matter how hard I cried or tried or prayed, I couldn't get my body to lay still. That night seemed to go on forever; I thought I was never going to see the sun rise.

Breakfast was at 7am down 2 flights of stairs. About 7:15 my door swings open and they told me "This isn't the Hilton, if you want breakfast you're going to have to get up and go get it." I looked at the staff member and smiled and said I would gladly get up and go but I was going to need a cane or walker because after having muscle spasms all night I could barely get the few feet to my bathroom little lone down 2 flights of stairs. She just looked at me and told me that wasn't going to happen, that they weren't a medical facility but a rehab facility and told me again to get up and get to breakfast. So I did as I was asked. As the staff stood there and watched me I got up and took a couple of steps and hit the floor. She just stood there and looked at me as my legs shook. She then helped me up and back to my bed and went and got their nurse. I think they thought I was just trying to be difficult but I was just doing all that I could. Their nurse came in an evaluated me and had me again try to stand again and after realizing that I wasn't going to be able to go to breakfast she left the room to make some calls she said. It was about 15-20 minutes later she came back in and told me that I needed to get ahold of someone to come and get me or they were going to have me transported by ambulance to a hospital. Since they didn't have a wheelchair she went and got one of their desk chairs that was on wheels and wheeled me over to their phone on the desk. So I called Travis and told him to come and pick me up. He was floored because he had just brought me up there the night before, but he came up right away. He signed me out and had to take me to an ER. We went to my heart doctor's ER and they evaluated me and gave me a script for methadone, the medicine for withdrawals, and sent me home. So I went home and followed up with my doctors plus we went to family therapy for a couple three months to help the kids' process and understand everything that had gone on. I had missed my kids' birthday family celebrations, school concerts, parent meetings, sporting events, etc. Plus I almost always stayed home while the rest of my family would go out and do things together. My kids weren't even able to, at the worst of times, even carry on a conversation with me.

I felt horrible, like the worse mom of the year award right here. When I would get down on myself, Satan was always right there, hitting the replay over again and again reminding me of all the things I had done wrong. Reminding me of the Christmas that my older brother and his family were back from California for Christmas, I had planned to take everyone shopping but instead I gave them the money and the keys to my car and they went without me.

The therapist also said I suffered from PTSD(Post Traumatic Stress Disorder) due to things that had happened to me growing up. I went from an angry and intimidating father to being molested by my neighbor, from a step-dad who made my life difficult for me to the point that I ended up in a foster home till I was emancipated at the age of 16 as the state released me to myself making me my own legal guardian. It was then that I became pregnant and miscarried twins my junior year of high school. The list goes on and Satan knows it and gladly reminds me of my past and mistakes every chance he has.

With time, and still continuing to this day, I work with giving things over to God. That was hard for me to do at the beginning. Give it to God and not worry about it. I didn't understand it at first. I would pray and ask the Lord to take these issues from my mind and to help me to forgive myself. In the beginning it was like, okay I said the prayer, I talked to God like He asks me to and He supposed to take these things away but I am still stewing over the things I just asked for help from. The more I attempted to do this it seemed the more frustrated I would get. Then one day, it was like a switch turned on. God gently reminded me that I am not like Him. When I have done wrong or something bad has happened, I can ask Christ for forgiveness. The Bible states "*I, even I, am He who blots out your transgressions, for my own sake, and remembers your sins no more.*" Sins are no longer "kept on file", record is blotted out, destroyed. God cannot "forget" like in human error, but He chooses to "not remember." **Isaiah 43:25**.

Then God reminded me "*As far as the east is from the west, so far has He removed our transgressions from us.*" **Psalm 103:12**. "*Surely the arm of the Lord is not too short to save, or his ear too dull to hear, but your iniquities have separated you from your God; your sins have hidden his face from you, so that He will not hear.*" **Isaiah 59:1-2**. Then God gave me this "*For if you forgive men when they sin against you, your heavenly Father will also forgive you. But if you do not forgive men their sins, your Father will not forgive your sins.*" **Matthew 6:14,15.**

So basically, I am not going to be able to forget all the things that happened to me because I am not God. And forgiving others is not for them but for me, if I live in the hurt and the past Satan will help it consume me. So in the end, I give everything to the Lord, I am a sinner and will mess up every day of my life. But I am not going to give my time to dwell on things I can't change. I just stay good with God, and by doing that everything else falls into place. I remembered "If God is for us, who can be against." Romans 8:31. With the Lord on my side what can anyone do to me?!? I have to remind myself of this even today because as long as I live here on this earth I have to deal with man and be ready to handle Satan at any given time. But I know I am not alone… EVER!!!

6

Now that I was back to a clean slate I guess you could say. The doctors starting trying to put my medication part of my life back together. Taking me off this and putting me on that or substituting one med for another. At one point in time I was taking up to 15 different medications daily. Then my body started to react to all the adding and subtracting and switching the doctors were doing and that's when I started having one medical issue right after another. First off my PFO, (Patent foramen ovale) is a hole between the left and right atria (upper chambers) of the heart that fails to close naturally soon after a baby is born, was the accompanying factor in my stroke. I got a blood clot and instead of going to my lungs, like it normally happens, it went through my PFO in my heart where it was sent straight to my brain. Never knowing I had this condition in my heart because I grew up as a very active and athletic kid. Well one of the issues that started was that my oxygen saturation (oxygen in your blood) was low and I was having problems sleeping at night because I wasn't getting enough air. The blood would go through that PFO and miss getting circulated through my lungs to get oxygen, so it was taking back un oxygenated blood to my body which cause stress issues for which I had been put on an oxygen machine to use at night to help with this issue. Then on top of that my blood pressure was dropping really low that it was putting me to sleep. After trying different methods finally everyone agreed that I needed to have surgery to fix my PFO.

This I would have to say was the scariest yet fascinating surgery I have ever had because I actually had to remain awake for the surgery as I had to participate in the procedure. They went in through my groin, which wasn't numb and rather painful for a few seconds. There were 4-5 screens on the wall to my left that showed every different angel and where they were. They had a few leads in my vessel and at first I didn't want to watch but I finally turned my head and started paying attention. They were going to be using this mesh type of closure to seal the PFO. The part they needed me for was to secure the closure seal. So they got the mesh closure on one part of the opening, remember I am watching them doing all this in there on a screen while my heart was just beating away, they got the piece in place and then asked me to give a couple really good coughs. When I coughed, the force made by a deep cough had the pressure needed to secure that closure in place. Then they had to go into the other side of the PFO and place a closure there as well, so it was sealed from both sides. So I waited till it was my turn again, coughed for them and secured the second side. The procedure went perfect and I was taken back to my room for recovery. They had to sandbag me down where they went in through my groin and I had to stay in that position with those bags for like 3-4 hours. Right away after hooking me back up to the monitors there was instant results. My oxygen saturation was 99-100 and my blood pressure was normal. My family even told that the color was back in my face and body and didn't look so pale and washed out as soon as they wheeled me back into my room. I thanked God right then and there, as it was obvious that he had been in that surgery room the whole time assisting the doctors with their very delicate work. My procedure was one of the first things right after lunch. They thought they would have to keep me over night because they had to make sure that vein was closed and then I had to be able to walk and go to the bathroom. It was 8-8:30 but I had met the requirements and things were going smoothly, so I was allowed to go home. That's always better than staying in the hospital.

My next adventure was after having a bad report from my yearly female screening which was showing very threatening pre-cancerous cells on my ovaries, uterus, basically the whole female reproduction organs. They wanted surgery as soon as possible because in just the short amount of time since they found them and were monitoring them they were growing rapidly. So I realized that having my tubes tied after Zach was a waste of money because now they were taking everything out. They cut me from stem to sternum. I had like 35-40 staples holding my mid-section together. The surgery had gone good, as they had gotten everything out but it wasn't till a couple of days later, I passed a large wad of gauze they had forgotten and left inside me. I remember passing it and part of the next day, then I only know what my family, friends and hospital staff told me. Travis told me that I starting running an extremely high fever and getting sick to my stomach, which was all being caused from the toxic shock. I guess Travis and the kids took me to the ER and that immediately wanted me

---

admitted. As the nurse, who was also my dear friend, was trying to get me admitted and an IV started Travis decided it would be best to get the kids home as it was in the evening when they took me over. I guess when they left I just started crying and begging them not to leave me there, taking out the IV and trying to go out the door to go with them. The nursing staff had to restrain me and restart the IV. My kids have told me that was the hardest thing they have ever had to do was leave me there begging for them not to leave me. I do not remember any of it, but if I could go back and take that horrible memory away I would in a heartbeat. I had been in the hospital for a couple of days before I finally came around and asked where I was and what was going on.

The next thing I know is that my body was starting to have issues again with blood pressure and becoming type 2 diabetic. I was gaining all kinds of weight and was unable to lose a pound. I was barely eating but my weight had more than doubled. With all these issues going on I went to my first heart doctor to see what he wanted to do. He basically told me that I was going to have to lose weight and watch my diet otherwise I was a dead woman walking. After talking to him, my family doctor and my neurologist it was brought down to me to have gastric-bypass surgery done. That was their solution and said it would fix all that was going wrong with me.

So Travis and I got onto the internet and started doing some research into gastric-bypass surgery and the best and most experience doctors closest to us. We found a wonderful clinic in Tulsa, OK. There was a guideline of requirements that I had to meet before the surgery could even be done. I had to meet with their nutritionist so many times, had to attend one of their support group meetings, and my BMI had to be at a certain level.

After jumping through all the hoops and talking with the surgeon about it he said my BMI just barely high enough for them to even consider doing it but after talking with all my other doctors the surgeon even agreed that it sounded like the best solution for my problems.

We scheduled the surgery and went down there for it because it was an overnight stay in the hospital. The surgery went just as hoped and I was given the all good and was told what to expect and what I needed to do for this to work. I followed all the directions. Before surgery I was a size 16-18 in women's. Under a year later I had dropped over 120 pounds and am now a size 8-10. I was back to wearing shorts and shirts I hadn't worn since high school. Not only that, but within a month my blood sugars had balanced out and they were normal and my type 2 diabetes was gone and my blood pressure been normal since. Finally at least for the time being things were getting close at as normal as things could get for me, for now anyways.

7

Now a while after processing and working through the loss of DeAnn, Arland getting remarried, we still had Justin, Sherame's husband, still in his battle with his bone cancer. To this day Travis says it was a miracle that day Justin came out to help them get the equipment unstuck, because if he hadn't injured his leg there and followed up with the doctor who knows when or if Justin would of caught it and been able to catch it in time to treat it. His cancer was found shortly after DeAnn's and they were both doing treatment at the same time. He went a year cancer free but they just knew their daughter, Kinze, was going to be their only child do to Justin's cancer treatment. I told Sherame that I didn't believe that. I told her I was going to be consistently praying for God to bless them with another baby. Sherame thought I had lost it and didn't see how it could be possible. She quit taking her birth control.

Several months had past and nothing had happened and every time I would see them I would tell Sherame that I was still praying. She would just smile and tell me, "Okay, you do that.", and of course I did.

Sherame and Justin, just like Travis and I, have a pretty normal life which means they are busy all the time. Sherame and I, needless to say, didn't talk too much and when we did it was usually always in person at a family get together.

I will never forget that morning. It was about 7am and our household was just getting around when the phone rang. It was Sherame and she was all excited. She told me, with overwhelming joy holding back tears, "Shannon, I'm pregnant!" I remember responding in the same type of loudness and excitement saying "YES!!! God is AWESOME!!" Of course by now everyone in the house was in my bedroom trying to figure out what in the world was going on. As my family sat around anxiously waiting for me to get off the phone, I just hung up and the tears just started rolling down my checks. Everyone was so ready to hear what was going on and it had sounded so happy they couldn't understand why I was crying. I told them it was good news and that they were tears of joy and told them that their Aunt Sherame was pregnant. The girls then joined me in my tears as we all had a little celebration there on my bed.

The celebration was short lived as unfortunately she had a miscarriage. I wouldn't wish that on anyone. I could empathize with her unfortunately, because when I was 16, a junior in high school, I got pregnant and miscarried twins. My grandma had always told me that she wouldn't want that for anyone but she saw it as a second chance for me because she knew I was in no way ready to be a parent. But this wasn't the situation for Sherame. We all wanted this. To show the doctors that they may have their theories but that God makes the final decision and determines the outcome of everything.

I felt bad because I felt like I was the one who kept getting her hopes up. But then I thought about it. Maybe things weren't quite ready yet for them to have another, or as my girls and I thought, maybe DeAnn ask to keep that part of them up there. Anyway you tried to explain it, it didn't fit into the desired that we all wanted for them.

But I refused to accept that and didn't believe that was it. God showed us He was in control and always had been and I knew all I had to do is pray for it without ceasing. God challenges us to test His word. God watches over His word to preform it. God's not a bully who likes to watch us suffer but wants us to come to Him in prayer with our requests and desires, but here's the tricky part, ready to accept His answer as it falls in according to His plan for us and not our own.

So, I kept praying, this time not bring the issue up, but I prayed for God to bless Justin, Sherame, & Kinze with a beautiful lil man to complete their family. That's what most women say, "I want one boy and one girl, one of each that way." Well that was the idea behind my plan. Show us all just what an awesome God you are and that even though it didn't go as we had planned the first time, that doesn't mean Your plan is over.

So I continued to pray for God to show His wonders. Honestly, I just really do get a kick out of God making all the doctors and professionals who have studied all these years and read all these books get their mind completely blown away.

So it was around Thanksgiving time. Justin and Sherame had this way about them. Sherame was just glowing, but hadn't lead onto anyone that anything was up, at least not me anyway. Finally as the evening started getting later I just couldn't help this feeling I had that something was up. That's when they shared with us that they were pregnant again!! I got all teary eyed and instantly told God "Thank you. All good things come from You! You're awesome!" Then I told Sherame that I had never stopped praying and we kind of joked that maybe DeAnn had put a little word in there for us too.

Sherame had a pretty normal pregnancy and on March 27, 2010, our family was blessed with its newest member Layne. He was perfect and healthy in every way! It was a miracle. The impossible became possible only by the hand of God. You know every now and then when I think about this and see that beautiful boy running around playing with all the kids, I picture God just looking down on Justin at his follow-up cancer appointment when he brings the whole family in with this precious little boy the doctor said wasn't even possible. I can just picture Christ with this smile on His face saying "Now, whatcha gonna say? Find that in your books and explain it!" And as the doctors stubble over themselves because most just think there has to be a reason or some sort of explanation. But the really good and great doctors always know the reason and how to handle it. They tell you that you've been touched by God and to Him be ALL the glory! I just love it when that happens!!!

8

Everyone's daily routine was going. Just the normal hustle of the average family routine: basketball, orthodontist, school events, etc. Simply just busy, busy, busy. During the 2010-2011 school year my daughters Jordyn, an 8th grader, and Macy, a 7th grader, were involved in everything. It went from cheerleading to volleyball to basketball then track, plus playing competitive basketball on top of it all. Their Jr. High basketball team had been awesome all season. At the end of one of the games the buzzer went off as Jordyn was going for a rebound. She came down and landed wrong breaking her ankle, actually it was an extra piece of bone that had grown off the side of another, anyway, that extra piece broke off and went into the tendon. Jordyn ended up having to have foot surgery. Not only to remove the piece of bone she broke off that was now in her tendon but she was also flat footed so our foot doctor was going to fix that foot's arch.

Before Jordyn had surgery her team was playing for League champs. She sat out a game, but being almost 6 ft.

tall the team needed her height. Macy is only an inch shorter. Anyways they lost the chance to play for 1st or 2nd but Jordyn decided that she was going to play through the pain in her foot to help her team. The doctor told us that she couldn't do anymore damage to it that it was up to her if she could handle the pain to play on it. So she played in the game they played for third and did what she could to help them win.

It came time for her surgery and I took her in as her foot surgery was an outpatient procedure. She came out of surgery loopy and her doctor and I walked her back to her room and he noticed how I was walking with my left foot as I didn't have a brace on and noticed that I was walking more on the side of my left foot than the bottom and asked me why I wasn't wearing an AFO (ankle foot orthotic). I explained that the one I had gotten one right after getting out of my in-patient rehab and that it rubbed on my leg causing it to rub and make you sweat because in goes under your foot and this one went up the back of my leg. It was made out of thick plastic that stuck to my leg and make my leg sweat which in turn would make it rub causing sores so I learned how to get along without using a brace or cane or any type of assistance.

As we continued the treatment on Jordyn, my walk continued to get worse. By the time she was completely back to 100% I was barely walking, so now it was my turn. I went in to see him to see what he could do. After evaluating me he decided what procedures he would do.

He went into my left foot/ankle and started by splitting my Achilles tendon, attaching some of it to the top of my foot to help with my foot drop because on my left side I am paralyzed from the ankle down, not being able to rotate my ankle, wiggle my toes or anything. It really sucks because I can't wear a lot of shoes I use to enjoy like flip flops & etc. Anyways after splitting and attaching that he then split the tendon on the side of my foot and attached part of it to the inside to pull my foot back straight. Anyway after about 15 anchors, staples, and stitches, my foot was back to a neutral position ready to be fitted for a new brace. The only thing is that after my surgery I had to be completely weightless for 6-8 weeks. Well I can't use crutches; those have no purpose when you only have use of one hand. The other one is just there to balance out the look. So the only option I had was a wheelchair.

So I got a standard wheelchair but the easiest thing for me to use was the electric wheelchair. So being permanently disabled, not only do I get the best parking spot but I qualified for a power chair. Then the task of going somewhere, the chair doesn't just fold and go so I had to get a ramp/lift that went on my vehicle. But I couldn't go by myself alone anywhere because I couldn't get to the back of my car weightless. I thank God for blessing me with such wonderful friends. As things came up like doctor appointments, grocery shopping, or just getting out of the house I always had someone who could usually take me as needed. After the wheelchair came the walking cast, then into a boot.

I got easily depressed because I couldn't really get up and do anything. Then I would have to remind myself not give in and let things get the best of me but instead let the best of me deal with all the things that I would face. I would be a liar if I said that I never gave into things. Of course, sometimes I would have quite a few in a row. Days where I wouldn't feel like getting out of bed and if I did it was just to the couch with the TV on and all shut up in my house. When Pastor Kurt would visit, he already knew I was down and out because he hadn't been seeing me at church or out and about. One time he stopped by and was like "man turn a light on it's like a dungeon in here." He always called it" stinkin thinkin", but he always would listen to me complain about how I couldn't run or play basketball with my kids anymore. I can't cross stitch or even just ride a bike or roller skate. I LOVED to roller skate when I was young and I always enjoyed cross stitching, I could get lost in that like someone gets lost in a book. Then after I was done saying what I had to say he'd always smile, which he has a smile that just makes you smile, and say it could always be worse. "I complained that I had no shoes till I met a man that had no feet." He always knew just what to say. Then I would smile and remind myself and him that even if I live to be 100 yrs old, that's nothing to the new body I get in eternity with Christ where none of the worries and problems of the world will ever exist.

I was blessed with the fact that when I married Travis, I married into a strong Christian family. His parents were high school sweethearts and together until his mom, DeAnn, passed away from breast cancer. Both sets of his Grandparents had also been together since school. His dad's mom was already passed by the time I came into the picture but I was lucky enough to get to meet Travis's Grandpa Dwight before he passed. His mom's parents were high school sweeties too! His Grandma Louise stepped in as Grandma since DeAnn was gone and my Grandma, my biological mom's mother, passed away from lymphoma and my biological dad's mom also was passed. But this isn't the Old Testament so besides Travis also losing both his Aunts to cancer, everyone left was a true blessing. We treasured his Grandma Miles (Louise) as long as we had her.

Grandma Miles (Louise) was always right there to teach me things that I am really glad I know now. She taught me how to garden and how to can things or make things like pickles, pickled beets, green beans and many other things I learned how to do. She added to my knowledge of cooking and we would swap recipes and family secrets. You always knew if she had stopped by while you were gone because there was always something like homemade banana bread, cookies, or something she might of whipped up for you.

Grandma Miles loved to garden and cook. Her and Travis spent a lot of time together working in the garden. She was a pro at using a hoe to weed out the beans. I've never seen someone attack beans the way she did with one but never hurt the beans. Her and Grandpa use to have a system. She would get up in the morning early while it was cooler and she would pick beans, and he would be waiting at the end of the row and as she brought him a bucket of beans, he would start snapping then and putting them in a bucket of water. It was so cute but also such a joy to watch Grandma and Grandpa interact. They were the perfect example of true love.

She and Trav would always have between 40-60 bean plants a year. That's not counting tomatoes, potatoes, beats, cucumbers, sweet corn, peppers of all kinds, cantaloupe, and watermelon plus anything else they might decide to try. Travis would also challenge her in making, canning, & trying new things. Sometimes it would be great and sometimes it would clear out the house. Like the time she was over helping Travis with his tomatoes. He had so many tomatoes that she would help him gather and sell 50lbs of tomatoes a week out of his garden. Well Travis had grown and dried out some cayenne peppers and decided that he was going to put them in a blender and grind them up to use them to shake and season food with. Grandma was in the basement laying out tomatoes on the table so they would start turning while Travis was stating this process upstairs. Trav said Grandma came out of that basement almost out of breathe and her eyes burning and watering. She told Travis they needed to get out of the house and get some air because those peppers were too potent.

Grandma and Grandpa had gotten them a Gator to get around on to go back and forth doing their gardening from the house. They have had that Gator for several years; there are pathways from the ways they most traveled. Grandpa Miles was one of the top horse breeders of his time. He was known for "Tamyon", she was one of the best

Travis had done some trimming and there had been trees cut down and stumps left in the yard. We all got use to going around them and never thought too much about it. Grandma already had arthritis really bad in her arm and hip and she was out on a beautiful morning doing what she loved, gardening. She had gotten done weeding around the beans and hopped into the Gator to head back up to the house and on her way out of the garden area she ran that Gator straight into a tree stump. She went on into the house and later came over to my house because she had made some banana bread she wanted to bring us. Grandma had been battling a cough for quite a few months now and when she came over to see me she sat down and coughed a little and told me what happened and that she was still pretty sore. I told her that we should go get checked out and she wasn't going to have it. She told me she would be fine and would keep me posted. Well the next day was only worse so finally she went in and got checked out. She had broken ribs and other problems and was admitted for a few days. She ended up going home and was still struggling with her breathing so the doctors had her on oxygen at home.

Well things just didn't seem to be getting any better so they readmitted her to the hospital and things had progressed to the point they were going to have to go in and do surgery. They hoped they could get in there without having to crack her chest open but once they got in there and looked at the situation they had no other route but to crack her chest and go through that way. They doctors said her lungs had fibrotic lung disease, which is where the lungs look like dried wood that could just be chipped away. They kept her comfortable in the hospital but there was nothing more there could be done. She passed away on September 16, 2011.

This was very hard on Travis; because he was a momma's boy then his mom passed away so Grandma Miles filled in that area of his life for him. Now losing her was hard on him along with his sister Sherame, and their cousins, who had also lost their mom to cancer. This family had been very close growing up together so it was a big loss. So we started preparing for her funeral. Little did I know that the day of her funeral would impact me in more ways than one!

9

It was the morning of Grandma's funeral, September 21, 2011, and everyone was getting ready we were running late and we were going to have to take 2 vehicles because we all couldn't fit into one. We were rushing out the door and my step daughter, Brooke, and I still had to put our shoes on and just planned on putting them on while we were going to the church. Well I was driving and Brooke was putting her shoes on. For some reason I started to head to our church on Main Street instead of Grandma's church in Milton, KS. Travis followed me and caught me at the corner by our bank at the stop sign and asked me what I was doing because I was heading to the wrong church. I told him I had a moment and that I would head that way. Well by now Brooke had her shoes on and I still needed to put my shoes on so Brooke and I switched places and I let her drive so I could put my shoes on. So Travis headed that way as Brooke and I switched places so we were a few minutes behind him.

I remember reaching down to the floor to grab one of my shoes and put it on and then waking up to a bunch of people in my face yelling and Travis tapping my face. I had no idea what was going on and a bit freaked out to come to with such commotion. Travis started asking me if I was okay and told me the ambulance was on the way. I was confused and wanted to know why the ambulance was coming. That's when he told me that I had just had a major grand mal seizure. I instantly thought of the kids, I thanked God that Brooke was driving and not me. I asked if they were okay and Travis told me that they were a little shook up. Jordyn had road over with him and so it was just Brooke, Macy, Zach and I in the car. Travis told me that Brooke pulled up in the middle of the street and was honking the horn and then got out of the vehicle hollering for help. He said my whole body was shaking and my eyes had rolled back into my head. Travis's cousin Michelle, her husband Kelly is a Fire Fighter from Wichita, one of the higher up helping with training, he was right there with Travis as I came to

I felt completely fine and we still had the service to go to. The ambulance showed up and they checked me out and were ready to transport me to a hospital. I thanked them for their concern but I felt fine and I wasn't about to miss Grandma's service. But since what was going on with me was considered life threatening they want to take me right away, but I refused the service because there was no way I was going to miss that service. I signed all their paper work and told them as soon as the funeral services were over I would get to a hospital right away. My girls were livid with me and wouldn't talk to me because I didn't go in the ambulance. I went on into the church for the service. Travis was a paul bearer, which they all sit together, but he was on the end and so they sat me next to him and my best friend Spring was right behind me. Everyone was really worried that I was going to have another seizure during the service but I didn't.

For the grave side service Spring drove me in my car and she stayed with me. I made it through the service and Spring and I had gotten back into my car and she was going to take me to the hospital to get check out. Well, when Spring and I are together we are always talking. I ended up having another grand mal seizure with her in the car with me. So she stopped in the middle of the road and called the ambulance. They took me to Hutchinson, KS hospital because that is where my neurologist was out of. So off to Hutch we went. Well I remember the ambulance ride to Hutch, they were evaluating me on the way up there and I told them that my tongue really hurt. They knew something had happened because they had to clean blood off my face. When checking out my mouth they saw the left side of my tongue was swollen out in one area about an inch. Well nothing like that happened the first time so I got to thinking, when the first one happened I was focused on putting my shoes on but during the second seizure I was with Spring chatting up a storm so when that 2nd seizure happened I was talking and my tongue was between my teeth when my jaw locked up.

They got me to Hutchinson Hospital and got me into the ER. I was laying there on the bed and different people were coming in and out of the room. Then something happened to me that I didn't know could even happen but I had a visual seizure and I remember every moment of it and it was really weird to say the lease. I will do my best to describe what I experienced: All of a sudden this picture came to mind and I could picture it and it was a picture of the holy trinity with this big man with a spear in his hand with long rolling white hair and beard all together and that represented God. Then there was this line that went to the cross with a crown of thorns on the top and then another line going down to a picture of Christ with His hands reaching out to welcome everyone. The picture was like a half of a diamond with God at top, cross out to the side the Jesus on the bottom. Then there were colors surrounding it and in my mind Jesus had come again and then I had to know the name of everyone that had helped me in the ER. So nurses that got me started and never came back I made them go get each person that had helped me because I had to know their name. They were all looking at me like I was crazy but this was what was going on in my head. As I learned their name I thanked God for them. Spring was sitting next to me telling me that everything was going to be okay.

Travis showed up at the end of it but saw what was going on and asked the doctor how this could be happening to me. They explained that because of my history of a stroke that I was more susceptible to having seizures and there are several different kinds of seizures and how they look when they happen can go to hardly even noticeable to severe. They also explained that medicines that I take could be also triggering the seizures as well. Travis wanted to know how I could be having the same reaction to all these different medicines. The doctor was explaining to both Travis and Spring that I might have been experiencing a visual seizures do to the damage that had occurred with the stroke to my brain and that there are many kinds of different seizures, three of which I had been having for years now and didn't know it. After the got everything stabilized they put me on a anti-seizure medication and sent me home with a scheduled follow up with my neurologist.

At my appointment with my neurologist I had brought a list of the current meds I was taken and he looked at the list and then looked at Travis and I had told us he had never seen a medicine list like mine. A lot of the medications I was taking were having interactions with some of the other medications. Plus with my history of stroke, any med that could have the side effect of a seizure I needed to stay clear from because of the damage to my brain from the stroke I was more probable to having seizures than someone who had never had a stroke. He got me lined out on my medications and sent us on our way with his final statement to me being that I couldn't drive again till I was seizure free for 6 months. That part was really a downer to me but I understood. There is no way I could ever live with myself if I got behind the wheel of a car and then had a seizure and wrecked and killed someone. That would completely devastate me. So even though I wasn't too fond of the news I completely abided by it.

This met instead of 6 weeks, like it was with my foot surgery, it was 6 months. During that time it was easy to get really down about things. Really easy! Since my stroke it takes me twice as long to do house work than it ever did, before I would have it done by noon and had the rest of the day to be with my kids. Now folding laundry has to be what I hate the worst, especially matching and folding socks. I would have to put them in my mouth to fold the together and that really sucked. Plus cleaning the bathroom, I would lose my balance. When trying to clean out the bath tub. Dishes wasn't so bad unless my family didn't rinse their dish, then trying to get off stuck on food to put them in the dishwasher just didn't work because I couldn't hold onto the dish while I was trying to wash it off that now most of my dishes are chipped or I broke them and had to replace them. But the most frustrating part was that I could bust my butt all day and when the kids are home from school and then in 5-10 minutes you could hardly tell I did anything and this really over frustrates me. Then if I would ask for help everything would become an argument from "I didn't make that mess" to "I had to do that last time" but the one that really hurt the most was when they would say "But what are you going to do"? Those words would just like instantly cut me to the bone. I knew they were just kids and being my kids they had grown up with me always being this way and it was hard for them to understand what it entailed for me to do the same things they could do without even thinking about it. Travis's Grandma Miles even tried to do like I do once by putting her hand in her pocket and not using it to do anything. She told me that "I couldn't do it for 5 minutes Shannon and I was already frustrated I quickly just took my hand out of my pocket and used it to get things done." I laughed and told her thanks for trying to understand my perspective and as she smiled back at me she told me "Yeah but you can't just take your hand out of your pocket and it will work." Yeah and that is my reality.

Anyway you looked at it; this was the situation I was in. I was good at sitting around and getting upset over the things I couldn't do that I really wanted to do instead of looking at what I had and do the best with what I could do. I realized that's the way God wanted me to look at things. I could do things, maybe not the same way as everyone else, but I could do it just the same. I had to quit letting situations or things I couldn't change ruin my day. As Pastor Kurt would start the saying "This is the day that the Lord has made and…" I would finish it by stating "… and I will rejoice and be glad in it." I felt like I had lost myself, my identity, because of what I couldn't do., which in some sense I had because I wasn't the same after my stroke. The problem was that I was identifying myself by what I could or couldn't do and not by who I was on the inside. I was still me on the inside but I had to learn how to get comfortable with the outside, and that's where my struggle was.

That's when I had to get my strength from Christ. I started by remembering and reminding myself of my favorite verse "I can do ALL things through Christ who strengthens me." **Philippians 4:13.** Another verse "*God is our refuge and strength, an ever-present help in trouble.*" **Psalm 46:1.** But this other verse helped a lot to, "*My grace is all you need. My power works best in weakness.*" So now I am glad to boast about my weaknesses, so that the power of Christ can work through me." **2 Corinthians 12:9.**

10

My life has finally started to balance out. My medications are down to just a few and instead of taking meds 4 times a day I now only take them twice a day. I am up and am active, going to all my kids' activities and sports I can. I still love going out with my friends for "Girls' Night" when we can all get together and just chat and watch movies or just spend time together.

I still have bad days and I know they are going to happen but I also know it depends on how I handle it on how the day goes. My girls are in high school now and before I know it they will be gone. Zach is just in third grade and does well.

There are still going to be changes and issues that I am going to have to face as I continue to get older. I will continue to have challenges that we will have to overcome and come through together. Life change is a process. It's a decision followed by a process. The apostle Paul said, to the Philippians, with total confidence, "I am certain that God, who began the good work within you, will continue his work until it is finally finished on the day when Christ Jesus returns" **Philippians 1:6**. If you have turned the changing process over to God and decided to work with God the best you can, God will work changes in you through the power of his Holy Spirit.

As I look back at my memories, I remember what my family always said about me, "Everything always happens to Shannon." which was true even growing up. I could never just get a scraped knee or anything simple; no it was things like falling off the rock wall around the Big Well Park in Greensburg and almost biting my tongue in half, for an true example. I look at that now and see that God had been trying to get my attention for a long time. God will make good out of any situation if you allow Him to. I finally realized that when I had my stroke and I wish I would have figured that out earlier. My Grandma would always tell me in times when I was struggling that when a situation brings you to your knees, that's where you should have started to begin with in dealing with it.

I don't share my story for sympathy or to make others feel bad because of everything I have gone though. I share my story to give hope to any and everyone who hears. So others can know of what I have been through that they themselves might be going through and realize that they are not alone but I can empathize with them because I have been there too. And if you can't figure out where to go and how to get through your struggle that maybe sharing how I got and continue to get through mine will help.

Each new day we are presented with a decision on how we are going to let our day go. We can choose to make it a good day, thank God for giving us a new day, and ask Him to help us and be with us through the day. Or we can choose to get up, have as Pastor Kurt would say "stinkin thinkin" and let our day be an all-day battle that we continuously try to get through by ourselves struggling every step of the way and end up mad and miserable at the end of the day. We each have to choose which direction we want each day to go as the sun rises on each new day.

I have also learned the importance of "true friends". Mine are Christians that believe in the same values that I do and are always there if something does go wrong. They will help pick me up when I fall and they never look down on me because of whatever I might be going through. They know if the situation was reversed I would be there for them. It doesn't matter if it's in the middle of the day and things have gotten overwhelming or if it's 2am and haven't been able to sleep and just need to talk to get things cleared out of your mind.

I know that I live on this world but am not of this world. I belong to Christ, as I am a sinner and will never be perfect; He died for my sins and rose from the dead giving me and everyone else who believes in Him eternal life. All I can say is "thank you Jesus for going and doing for me everything you have. I give God the glory for everything that has happened and continues to happen within my life and those around me. I thank you Lord for your guidance in writing this book and ask You Lord to use this to touch and bless other people through this book. I have personally witnessed Your miracles and cannot wait for You to come again and take us home. I thank you for each and every person who reads this and may their lives be blessed. I ask this all in Jesus name, Amen."

CPSIA information can be obtained at www.ICGtesting.com
Printed in the USA
LVOW060532161012

302962LV00002B/2/P